SOUTHERN HATRED

OF THE

AMERICAN GOVERNMENT,

THE

PEOPLE OF THE NORTH,

AND

FREE INSTITUTIONS.

BOSTON:
PUBLISHED BY R. F. WALLCUT,
No. 221 WASHINGTON STREET.
1862.

PREFACE.

This tract is supplemental to a tract of 24 duodecimo pages which was published last year by R. F. Wallcut, 221 Washington Street, Boston, entitled "*The Spirit of the South towards Northern Freemen and Soldiers defending the American Flag against Traitors of the deepest Dye.*" As far as practicable, both of these tracts should be carefully bound together for future reference, and as a matter of historical importance. To these should be added another, published by the American Anti-Slavery Society in 1860, entitled "*The Patriarchal Institution, as described by Members of its own Family—compiled by L. Maria Child.*"

All these tracts furnish overwhelming evidence, drawn from Southern sources, that it is not against Abolitionism or Republicanism, *per se*, but against free institutions and the democratic theory of government universally, that the South has risen in rebellion for the overthrow of the American Union, and the establishment of a hostile independent confederacy, based on oligarchic and despotic principles. The spirit by which she is animated, in her treasonable career, is comprehensively embodied in the following venomous statement of the *Richmond Examiner*: —

> "We have got to hating everything with the prefix *free*; from free negroes, down and up, through the whole catalogue. Free farms, free labor, free society, free will, free thinking, free children, and free schools, all belong to the same brood of damnable *isms*. But *the worst of all these abominations* is the modern system of *free schools*. The New England system of free schools has been the cause and prolific source of the infidelities and treasons that have turned her cities into Sodoms and Gomorrahs, and her land into the common nestling-places of howling bedlamites. We abominate the system, *because the schools are free*."

Also, in the following extract from the *Muscogee* (Alabama) *Herald*: —

> "*Free* society! We sicken of the name. What is it but a conglomeration of *greasy mechanics, filthy operatives, small-fisted farmers*, and moonstruck theorists? All the Northern States, and especially the New England States, are *devoid of society fitted for well-bred gentlemen*. The prevailing class one meets with is that of mechanics struggling to be genteel, and small farmers, who do their own drudgery; and yet who are hardly fit for association with a gentleman's body servant [slave]. This is your free society!"

What delusion or hypocrisy it is, then, to represent that the South has no objection to anything at the North but its Abolitionism! Read and ponder what she says of the Government, and of the People, Soldiers, and Institutions of the North!

SOUTHERN HATRED OF FREE INSTITUTIONS.

THOUGH last, not least, the new Constitution has put at rest forever all the agitating questions relating to our peculiar institutions—*African slavery* as it exists among us, the proper status of the negro in our form of civilization. *This was the immediate cause of the late rupture, and of the present revolution.* Jefferson, in his forecast, had anticipated this as the rock upon which the old Union would split. He was right. What was conjecture with him is now a realized fact. But, whether he fully comprehended the great truth upon which that rock stood, and stands, may be doubted. The prevailing ideas entertained by him, and most of the leading statesmen at the time of the formation of the old Constitution, were that the enslavement of the African race was in violation of the laws of nature; that it was wrong in principle, socially, morally, and politically. It was an evil they knew not well how to deal with; but the general opinion of the men of that day was, that, somehow or other, in the order of Providence, the institution would be evanescent, and pass away. * * * * *Those ideas, however, were fundamentally wrong. They rested upon the assumption of the equality of races. This was an error. It was a sandy foundation, and the idea of a government built upon it, when the storm came, and wind blew, it fell.*

Our new Government is founded upon *exactly the opposite ideas; its foundations are laid, its corner-stone rests, on the general truth, that the negro is* NOT *equal to the white man;* that slavery, subordination to the superior race, is his natural and normal condition. This, *our new Government, is the* FIRST *in the history of the world, based upon this great physical, philosophical and moral truth.* * * * * *

The negro, by nature or the curse of Canaan, is fitted for the condition which he occupies in our system. The architect, in the construction of a building, lays the foundation with the proper material—the granite—then comes the brick or the marble. The substratum of our society is made of the material by nature best fitted for it, and by experience we know it is best, not only for the superior but the inferior race, that it should be so. It is, indeed, in conformity with the Creator. It is not for us to inquire into the wisdom of His ordinances, or to question them. * * * * *

The great objects of humanity are best attained when conformed to His laws and decrees in the formation of governments, as well as in all things else. Our Confederacy is founded on principles in strict conformity with these laws. THIS STONE, WHICH WAS REJECTED BY THE BUILDERS, IS BECOME THE CHIEF STONE OF THE CORNER OF OUR NEW EDIFICE.

* * * * * *

These people are now warring against that principle, and attempting to govern us as King George did; it is, therefore, an unnatural and irrational and a suicidal war, and you cannot count upon its duration. When a people becomes mad, there is no telling what they will do. It is so in the history of other empires; it was so in France. They say we are revolutionists; they call us rebels. I think it will be a revolution before it is over; but if a change of government makes revolution, the revolution is at the North.

I tell you the revolution is at the North. There is where constitutional liberty has been destroyed; and if you wish to know my judgment about the history of this war, you may read it in the history of the French Jacobins. They have become *a licentious and cowardly mob*, and I shall not at all be surprised if, in less than three years, the leaders in this war, if Lincoln and his Cabinet, its head, came to the gallows or guillotine, just as those who led the French war; for human passions, when once aroused, are as uncontrollable as the elements above us. The only hope of mankind rests in the restraints of constitutional law, and the day they framed and ratified these lawless measures of Lincoln, they dug their own graves. They may talk of freedom and liberty, but I tell you no people without rulers restrained by constitutional law can be free. They may be nominally free, but they are vassals and slaves, and this unbridled mob, when they attempt to check it, Lincoln and the rest will be dealt with just as I tell you it was in France.—*Extracts from a speech of Alexander H. Stephens, Vice-President of the Confederacy.*

"Liberty or Death!" This was the cry of Patrick Henry in the great struggle for our national independence. We believe, at this moment, it animates the hearts of all true Virginians. Indeed, we have never seen nor imagined anything comparable in the feeling which pervades this Commonwealth at this time. Since the foul invaders have polluted our soil with their footsteps, an irrepressible eagerness to give them bloody graves pervades all classes. Old and young, women and children, all share in the exciting and universal emotion. Death to the tyrants is not only on the lips, but in the hearts of our whole population. The restraints of military discipline are scarcely thought of in the intense and restless anxiety to rush on the foe, and avenge in blood the outrage on our honor and freedom.

We confess to a thorough sympathy with this patriotic ardor, and know no refreshing sleep on account of the restless desire to be butchering the invading ruffians. But it is an impatience which we know should be moderated, and reduced to subordination to military discipline. Its unrestrained indulgence may bring more mischief on ourselves than on the enemy. We fear some such catastrophe. Let us, while we cherish an ardor and determination to resist to the death, remember that we have able military leaders, and put implicit confidence in the wisdom of their measures. *They are cheerful and confident at the prospect before us.* Let not the people be discouraged by any petty and temporary reverses that may befall us. The enemy have some advantages to start with; but we have advantages—the advantages of a brave and free people fighting for their firesides and freedom—against which all the hosts of despotism cannot prevail. We may be worsted to-day, but, cheered by

Liberty's manly voice, we will rally with redoubled energy for the fight to-morrow.

Let the bright example of Jackson of Alexandria animate every heart, and the memory of his sad fate impel the avenging steel of every Virginian. See in every Yankee the murderer of that patriot martyr!—*Richmond Whig.*

Do these besotted fanatics flatter themselves that Alexandria is to be kept in chains, like those which bind poor Baltimore to the car of the Federal despotism? The "bloody and brutal" purpose of the Abolitionists, to subjugate and exterminate the Southern people, stands confessed by this flagrant outrage upon Virginia soil.

Virginians, arise in your strength, and welcome the invader with "bloody hands to hospitable graves." The sacred soil of Virginia, in which repose the ashes of so many of the illustrious patriots who gave independence to their country, has been desecrated by the hostile tread of an armed enemy, who proclaims his malignant hatred of Virginia because she will not bow her proud neck to the humiliating yoke of Yankee rule. Meet the invader at the threshold. Welcome him with bayonet and bullet. Swear eternal hatred of a treacherous foe, whose only hope of safety is in your defeat and subjugation.

Virginia will be the Moscow of the Abolitionists—our armies are gathering to the prey, and so surely as the patriot-freemen of the Southern army come in conflict with *the mercenary hordes of the North,* so surely will they give the world another example of the invincibility of a free people fighting on their own soil for all that is dear to man.—*Richmond Enquirer.*

We rejoice at the death of Ellsworth, and only regret that every man who followed him did not share his fate; we lament the sacrifice of the gallant Virginian. * * * We trust that every colonel in the Federal service will meet his Jackson, and that every Hessian will find his grave upon her soil.—*Lexington (Ky.) Statesman.*

Our Women and Children. The newspaper organs of Lincoln are constantly fulminating the most atrocious threats against the women and children of the South. They tell us that these tender objects of our hearts' dearest affections are to be *subjected to indiscriminate massacre, and to outrage worse than death.* With fiendish satisfaction they gloat over the anticipated ruin of Southern homes, and the murder of the helpless and innocent.

These cowardly threats are neither disavowed nor rebuked by the Washington Administration. They are suffered to pass uncontradicted as authentic expositions of their purpose and policy. They are read by Lincoln's soldiers, as incentives to deeds of cowardly cruelty, and intimations of the blood-thirsty wishes of their employers. They will not be lost on *the rabble of vagabonds and cut-throats enlisted by Lincoln's agents, to execute his foul purposes.* We cannot doubt that they will be faithfully executed by these minions of the Administration, if they get an opportunity. *The drunken ruffian* who heads this degraded Administration, and the imbecile but wicked men who compose it, are perfectly willing to turn loose on the South these armies of mercenaries, with instructions to spare neither age nor sex.

A government that begins a war upon those whom it claims to be its own subjects, with the avowal of such atrocious designs, merits only the abhorrence and execrations of mankind, and puts itself outside the pale of civilized and Christian powers. Repudiating the merciful code of modern warfare, by which all Christian governments are restrained in the conduct of war, it classes itself with the Thugs and Sepoys of India, and the merciless savages of America, and is entitled to no more respect or quarter.

Abe Lincoln and his minions think to frighten the Southern people into submission by these horrible threats, but they only rouse them to more determined resistance. Southern men will only fight with more desperate valor, knowing that they are battling for their wives and little ones, whose lives are threatened by an atrocious and insolent invader. They will meet Lincoln's mercenaries on the field of battle as they would robbers and murderers assailing the safety and sanctity of their homes. They give the atrocious Washington cliques full credit for sincerity, in their avowed wish and intention to wage a war of extermination against the Southern women and children, but instead of being exterminated, they are only exasperated to wage against them an uncompromising war.

The Southern people are now satisfied that there was no safety for them under Lincoln's Government, and that they have not thrown off its yoke any too soon. Those who were inclined to judge it leniently, and to tolerate it longest, now see that it is the bitter and unscrupulous enemy of their section, aiming at the degradation and enslavement of the South, and *capable of any deed of hellish perfidy, of atrocious cruelty, of damning infamy*, to accomplish its ends. Since it has thrown off the mask, and shown itself in its true colors, exhibiting its real purposes, and the unparalleled treachery, injustice, oppression and unkindness of which it is capable, it has awakened in the breast of all true Southern men feelings of unutterable loathing and contempt, and of undying hatred. Upon the altar of their country they have sworn eternal enmity to the detested tyranny—none the less detested that it dares to threaten, with dastardly cowardice and inconceivable meanness, the safety and lives of our women and babes. —*Memphis Avalanche.*

The Northern people have gone mad—stark, staring, raving mad. As to New York city, it is nothing better than a vast mad-house. In no other way can their extraordinary and unparalleled circumsaltation be explained, in no other way can the supremacy gained by their brutal and bloody instincts over their boasted enlightenment and humanity be excused or extenuated. There is no doubt that the Northern people are at this moment fit representatives of the barbarian hordes which formerly devastated the world. They are furnishing the very best evidences that they are incapable of thorough civilization; that they possess only the outward symbols of modern enlightenment, while they are, by nature, cruel, blood-thirsty, arrogant and boastful. But there is really very little danger to be feared from them. Civilization no longer stands in dread of barbarism. One race of savages has already been expelled from the country; but not that it may fall into the hands of another.—*New Orleans Delta.*

About 1850, when the great northeastern deluge, of which mention has been made, swept over our commonwealth and laid waste our long-cherished institutions, it was very much the fashion for the "dear friend of the people" to hold up the Yankees as the models of every virtue. They were the thriftiest, the shrewdest, the 'cutest, the most enterprising, the most industrious, and the most money-getting people in the world. But their wealth, their stinginess, their venality, their dexterity paled before their unmatchable fecundity. Behold how they multiply! They are as multitudinous as the stars in the heaven, or the sand on the sea-shore. Malthus, never a favorite with the sentimentalist, though teeming with profoundest wisdom, was universally discarded as a humbug and charlatan. The great Yankee nation, which doubles itself every five years, was the true exemplar of all political science, and the only model of political greatness. It is very true that the Yankees are, without a doubt, eminently endowed with the procreative faculty. Their men are lecherous as monkeys, and the women, scraggy, scrawny and hard as whip-cord, breed like Norway rats, and they fill all the brothels on the continent. It is not presumable that the tender emotions of love ever penetrate their bony bosoms; but they indulge passion because it smacks of the savor of forbidden fruit, which is sweet to their sinful natures. But they multiply,—the only scriptural precept they obey,—and boast their millions. So do the Chinese; so do the Apisdæ, and all other pests of the animal kingdom. Pull the bark from a decayed log, and you will see a mass of maggots full of vitality, in constant motion and eternal gyration, one crawling over one, and another creeping under another, all precisely alike, all intently engaged in preying upon one another, and *you have an apt illustration of Yankee numbers, Yankee equality, and Yankee prowess.*

This war will test the physical virtues of mere numbers. Southern soldiers ask no better odds than one to three Western, and one to six of the Eastern Yankees. Some go so far as to say that, with equal weapons and on equal grounds, they would not hesitate to encounter twenty times their number of the last. In respect to administrative talent, the world has never seen such a failure. With a Government thoroughly organized in their hands, complete in all its branches, they have well-nigh smashed the whole concern in less than twelve months. So numbers do not make either warriors or statesmen.

In regard to the moral, the effects are by no means encouraging. We doubt if any society *since that of Sodom and Gomorrah* has ever been more thoroughly steeped in every species of vice *than that of the Yankees.* Infanticide is one of the established customs of the oriental Chinese; and it is by no means certain that it has not extensive prevalence among their brethren of the moral North. But this imputation need not be laid to their charge: they are bad enough without it. There is no one virtue cherished among them, except money-getting, if that can be called a virtue, pursued as it is by them to the stifling of every sentiment of generosity and honor. With envy and malignity, they pursue every excellence that shows itself among them, unconnected with money; and a gentleman there stands no more chance of existence than a dog does in the Grotto del Cano. —*Richmond Whig.*

WHEN the Yankees go to Lord John Russell, and tell him that *Virginia*, which inaugurated civilization and freedom on this continent, is one of *their* rebel provinces—why, his lordship, who is as thin-visaged as a razor and as scant of flesh as an Egyptian mummy, will give them a grin, which will last them a lifetime. *They*, the makers and venders of tin cups and wooden clocks, the liege lords of the Old Dominion—the sovereign and independent State of Virginia! If anything could inflame the indignation and scorn which this atrocious war excites, it would be this Yankee pretension to superiority and supremacy. To be under the dominion of a lady, like Queen Victoria, distinguished by every virtue, would constitute a favorable exchange for the vulgar rule of a brutish blackguard, like Lincoln. To be conquered in open and manly fight by a nation of gentlemen, and subjected to their sway, might not drive us raving distracted with rage and shame; but for Yankees—*the most contemptible and detestable of God's creation*—the vile wretches, whose daily sustenance consists in the refuse of all other people—for they eat nothing that anybody else will buy

— for them to lord it over us — the English language must be enlarged, new words must be invented, to express the extent and depth of our feelings of mortification and shame. No, it is not possible that we can be reduced to a state which there are no words to describe. Instead of this, we must bring these enfranchised slaves back to their true condition. They have long, very properly, looked upon themselves as our social inferiors — as our serfs; their mean, niggardly lives — their low, vulgar, and sordid occupations, have ground this conviction into them. But, of a sudden, they have come to imagine that their numerical strength gives them power — and they have burst the bonds of servitude, and are running riot with more than the brutal passions of a liberated wild beast. Their uprising has all the characteristics of a ferocious servile insurrection. Their first aim is demolition — the destruction of everything which has the appearance of superior virtue, which excites their envy and hate, and which, by contrast, exposes the shameful deformity of their own lives. They have suggested to us the invasion of their territory, and the robbery of their banks and jewelry stores. We may profit by the suggestion, so far as the invasion goes — for that will enable us to restore them to their normal condition of vassalage, and teach them that cap in hand is the proper attitude of the servant before his master. A cock for a sailor, a goose for a soldier — a Yankee for a gentleman — images incongruous and unnatural!!! — *Richmond Whig.*

Abe Lincoln is a fit successor and representative of the cruel king who thirsted for the blood of the infant Jesus. His cowardly and murderous heart prompts him to wreak his mean and hellish spite upon helpless children, rather than to encounter men in open and manly fight. He will never be caught in that scrape; he will sooner fly than face an enemy. * * * We would be guilty of injustice to the doomed spirits of hell, were we to style these assassins of infants fiends, demons, or devils. Those apostate angels, we may well believe, have too much pride to wreak their immortal hate on such victims. A respectable devil would blush at such a crime. — *Memphis Avalanche.*

THE rout and dispersion, at the great pitched battle near Manassas, bring into bold relief the great fact, that *the Yankees are humbugs*, and that the *white people* of the slaveholding States are the true masters—the real rulers of this continent. Under every disadvantage on our side, the preparations for the combat were made. The Northern States had seized upon all the common property of the partnership, had monopolized the whole navy and army, and all the material, with the entire machinery of government in full operation; and boasted that they had an inexhaustible supply of men and money to wage an interminable war. For months, with all these advantages, they have been diligently engaged in organizing their forces.

Under the direction of the most vaunted military character of the age,—not of their creation, though, for they never produced a genius capable of anything beyond arranging a hotel or working a steam engine, or directing some mechanical contrivance,—they expended millions of money and drilled armies of three hundred thousand, and equipped them in a style unheard of in the annals of war. They met the rude and poorly equipped *volunteers* of the Southern States, drawn from their peaceful vocations for the first time, to the theatre of war, and they are routed and slain by the thousand, and driven like chaff before a high wind. Though guided by the highest military talent, (of Virginia short-grass growth,) they have nothing to rely upon but their numbers, and that, in the fight, proves an element of weakness.

The fact is, the Yankees are very little better than the Chinese. They lay the same stress on the jingle of their dollars that the Celestials do on the noise of their gongs. Originally endowed with no single amiable trait, they have cultivated the arts of money-getting and cheating, until gain has become their God, and they imagine it to be omnipotent. With money in their pockets, won from a generous and chivalrous race, and multitudinous as Norway rats, they are swollen with conceit, and fancied that they were fit for empire. And yet they do not possess one gentlemanly attribute, nor a single talent that qualifies them for war. Of the very first element they are destitute. They don't even know how to ride a horse—a talent only to be acquired in youth, amid gentle avocations. And as to arms, ninety-nine out of a hundred never shot a gun; and we have it on very good authority that Old Scott lost all patience in attempting to teach them how to load a gun. The vile old wretch! he reaps a just reward for his treason and his talents misapplied.

The break down of the Yankees, their utter unfitness for empire, forces dominion upon us of the South. We are compelled to take the sceptre, and it is our duty to prepare ourselves for our destinies. We must elevate our race, every man of it—breed them up to arms, to command—to empire. The art military should constitute a leading part of every white man's education. The right of voting should be a high privilege, to be enjoyed by those only who are worthy to exercise it. In a word, the whole white population of the South should be brought into a high-toned aristocracy, duly impressed with a sense of its own functions, and its obligations to freedom and civilization.—*Richmond Whig.*

Lincoln's War Policy. The policy which dictated and directs the war now waged by the North against the South is one of unmatched and unmitigated atrocity. The ordinary sentiments of humanity and the benevolent principles of the Christian religion are stifled and ignored. Schemes of hellish cruelty and outrage, such as never before were conceived by the most bloody tyrants or relentless savages, are freely and shamelessly discussed and advocated by the satanic press of the North; and an administration, whose folly is only surpassed by its intense and boundless wickedness, hastens to adopt and carry into execution these diabolical counsels.

Lincoln's programme of this war presents, as its most prominent features, indiscriminate massacre and pillage, the murder of defenceless women and unoffending children, the sacking and burning of Southern homes, towns and cities, the extermination of an entire people, and the utter desolation of a land, whose inhabitants are guiltless of any crime, save the assertion of the sacred right of self-government, bequeathed to them by their fathers.

A brutal soldiery, raked from the sewers of vice and crime, the scum of the population of Northern cities, and a servile race to be incited to insurrection, have been selected as the instruments to carry out this *peace* programme of the infamous Lincoln and his junta of co-assassins. The Lincoln organs, appealing to *the brutal instincts of the ruffian minions of despotism, sent to subjugate the South*, tell them that "beauty and booty" shall be their reward; that to each of them shall be parcelled out one hundred and sixty acres of the confiscated lands of Southern planters, with a slave to wait upon him; that a gold watch, filched from the pocket of a murdered Southerner, shall be thrown in as a perquisite, and that license will be given them to pillage whatever they can lay their hands upon, and to burn and butcher *until their savage natures shall be satiated with vengeance and blood.*

This is no fancy sketch, but *a truthful outline of the code of instructions to Lincoln's troops*, reiterated by the Northern newspapers from day to day. The government which has projected and is seeking to carry out this scheme of stupendous crime, is one professing to have been instituted for the good, and to derive all its just powers from the consent of the governed — the paternal guardian of the safety and rights of those whom it conspires to rob and murder. — *Memphis Avalanche.*

The Chinese and the Yankees are exceedingly alike, and we have always thought that they were much more nearly related than the Japanese and the almond-eyed people of the Flowery Kingdom.

When a Chinaman prepares for war — measuring his enemy's courage by his own — he attempts to work upon his fears. He puts on a hideous mask, arms himself with a huge shield, upon which he paints some unearthly monster; and, when thus accoutered, he goes forth in cold sweat to encounter the enemy. As soon as he beholds his adversary, he utters a fearful roar, broadsides his shield, and if his opponent does not at once take to his heels, John Chinaman always does.

The wars of New England have always been conducted upon the Chinese plan. To hear their orators and read their newspapers, one would suppose that he was looking at a Chinaman clothed with all the pomp and circumstance of mask, shield, and stink-pot. The Yankee orators are only equalled by the Yankee editors in deeds of valor. Let war be breathed, and the first swear to a man that they are ready and anxious to exterminate creation, whilst the latter, not content, like Alexander, to sigh for more worlds to conquer, threaten to destroy the laws of gravity, and lay violent hands upon the whole planetary system. Yet, these war mandarins are all members of the Peace Society, and would no more think of resenting a blow on the cheek, the seduction of a wife, or the dishonor of a daughter, than they would of flying. We have not forgotten how all Massachusetts collected in Boston, when Anthony Burns was to be delivered to his Virginia master, and swore that it should not be done. A single file of soldiers, however, marched the fugitive from State street to the lower end of Long Wharf, through miles of streets packed with valorous fanatics, who did nothing but sing old Puritan hymns, with a most hideous and barbarous disregard to metre.—*Richmond Examiner.*

John Forsyth, editor of the Mobile *Register*, vents his indignation upon the North in this way:—

"The cry of the North is for war! War to save the Union, to defend the United States flag, 'to show that we have a government.' These are the pretences of sheer hypocrisy. They are the patriotic gloss given to a false cause. The cement that unites the North is rage at the inevitable mischief that has been done to Northern property by the loss of the trade and tribute of ten, perhaps twelve, of the richest and most productive States of the late Union.

"If they want war, give it to them to their heart's content—to the knife and the hilt. Give them battle every morning and every evening, whenever we can marshal a force for the fight. Nor should we stop to receive it. It ought to be sought for and invited. Nor wait to drive them from confederate soil, but force the war to their own borders. We hold that the enemy should be driven from Washington—not because we want Washington, but because it is in a slave State, and because our brethren in Maryland should be released from the iron heel of military power that is upon their necks. Whose blood does not boil to read of the proud men of Maryland overrun and subdued by the outcasts of Massachusetts, under the lead of that scoundrel, Gen. Butler, who played his part in the political disturbances that were the immediate cause of this revolution? Maryland should be freed at all hazards, and the enemy driven beyond the Susquehanna.

"Defensive aggression is the Southern policy in this war. The surest and the safest way to defend our homes is to meet the enemy at a distance from them—to keep away the havoc and devastation of conflict from our women and children as far as possible. The North has undertaken to conquer the South. We must make up our minds to conquer the North, at least so far as to dictate the terms of peace. To this end, every man must devote himself to arms. Nothing else is of value, nothing worthy to be thought of in comparison to the sacred duty of defending the liberties of our country in this atrocious war. We must become a nation of soldiers, and every man ready to take the field when called upon. An active and desperate war is always a short one. We cannot make this war too bloody or too desperate."

THEY are alarmed for Washington, but they have not yet begun to tremble for New York and Boston. As England and France knew that there would be no stable peace with the treacherous, knavish, cowardly and cruel Chinese, short of Pekin, so we know that there can be no lasting peace with the *Chinese counterparts* on this continent until Confederate cannon overawe New York, and Confederate legions *bivouac on Boston Common.* Boston is the Pekin of the Western China; and "On to Pekin" is the watchword of Southern armies. Washington is a mere circumstance. We don't want it, any further than to dislodge the *obscene birds* that now infest it. Baltimore, too, which inspires the tyrants with so much terror, is not worth a moment's consideration—beyond breaking the fetters (in passing) of that outraged people. Our true goal is *Pekin*—the headquarters of *the genuine Tartar horde, with their gongs and stink-guns.* The military occupation of the Yankee capital can alone give indemnity for the past and security for the future. Then up with the universal shout, "ON TO PEKIN!"—*Richmond Whig.*

The rapidity with which Northern society has been demoralized is almost incredible. All the domestic relations are affected by it; husband and wife, parent and child, live together there, or rather apart, in a manner which is an outrage in the sight of Heaven, and of the great Eye of Humanity. We do truly hold that it is, perhaps, from utter despair at a state of things of which they seem at once the unavoidable occasion, if not cause, and the victims, that so many of the better sex have singly, or in bands, perpetrated of late years so many extravagancies in that region. They deserve pity rather than condemnation. * * *

The system of education at the North, which is being introduced among us, has been much criticised, and with justice. It contains much that is bad. Indeed, contemplated in some of its aspects and relations, particularly with reference to its effects, we do not think we go further than truth warrants, when we say that it would be a curse in any country. * * * *

It is very evident, to many of those who are at all conversant with the details of life at the North, that the people of that section are, whether from the effects of climate acting upon the idiosyncracy of race, or from some other cause, wonderfully predisposed to insanity. Legislators, theologians, judges, lawyers, physicians, merchants, in very respectable standing, have exhibited characteristics, and used language and performed actions, indicative of a morbid condition of the functions usually attributed to the brain. Here is a society almost wholly touched with an epidemic mental disorder of such a nature as to seem contagious. The very crimes that are committed in all that part of the Union, when not the acts of acknowledged madmen, have something about them in the details and circumstances of their development which similar crimes of other culprits never exhibit. —*Richmond Literary Messenger.*

If the hungry and ravenous pack of hyenas who are sent upon their hellish missions of plunder and rapine are driven back into their dens, they will turn upon their silly betrayers, only to make them the victims of their devouring wrath.—*Memphis Appeal.*

The experiment of republican institutions is lost at the North, and it can only be saved at the South by maintaining as strict non-intercourse with *the moral Sodom and political Pandemonium on our borders* as the nature of the case will permit. We are willing to agree to the cessation of hostilities; but if any foreign mediation shall exact concessions of intercourse, and commercial and political privilege, as a bargain and stipulation, it will exact what cannot be granted without destruction to our social, political and commercial integrity.

The case, therefore, is not one for arbitration. The South cannot refer so grave a question as that of her independence to any arbitration, much less to that of a foreign potentate. Did ever two litigants refer to arbitration the question of either one's slavery? Independence is a question that cannot be referred by the South, and that is, in fact, the only question really involved in the present contest. The Yankee may become sick of the war, and is capable of descending from a demand of our service and fealty to begging the privilege of peddling his wooden nutmegs and bark clocks through our country; but neither of these demands are proper for mediation, and we should be very wary of granting treaty privileges of trade. Despairing of conquering the South by open hostilities, they will try the artifice of the Greeks before Troy, and attempt to introduce, by means of trade privileges, the wooden horse into our midst. It is only some purpose of this sort that mediation can accomplish; and we should distrust and eschew such schemes, as the Trojans learned to distrust their enemies, even when bearing pretended gifts.—*Richmond Dispatch.*

The New Orleans *Advocate*, a religious paper, of which Rev. C. C. Gillespie, D. D., is editor, says:—"Davis is the very soul of courage, honor, chivalry; Lincoln is a cowardly sneak. In the midst of the present storm, Davis is calm, cool, generally cheerful, comprehensive in observation, rigidly keeping his own counsel. Lincoln is filled with abject fear, *drunk half the time, occasionally foolishly facetious, whistling to keep his courage up!*"

When a long course of class legislation, directed not to the general welfare, but to the aggrandizement of the Northern section of the Union, culminated in a warfare on the domestic institutions of the Southern States—when the dogmas of a sectional party, substituted for the provisions of the constitutional compact, threatened to destroy the sovereign rights of the States—six of those States, withdrawing from the Union, confederated together to exercise the right and perform the duty of instituting a government which would better secure the liberties, for the preservation of which that Union was established.

Whatever of hope some may have entertained that a returning sense of justice would remove the danger with which our rights were threatened, and render it possible to preserve the Union of the Constitution, must have been dispelled by *the malignity and barbarity of the Northern States in the prosecution of the existing war.* The confidence of the most hopeful among us must have been destroyed by the disregard they have recently exhibited for all the time-honored bulwarks of civil and religious liberty. Bastiles filled with prisoners, arrested without civil process or indictment duly found; the writ of *habeas corpus* suspended by Executive mandate; a State Legislature controlled by the imprisonment of members whose avowed principles suggested to the Federal Executive that there might be another added to the list of seceded States; elections held under threats of a military power; civil officers, peaceful citizens and gentle women incarcerated for opinion's sake, proclaimed the incapacity of our late associates to administer a government as free, liberal and humane as that established for our common use.

The people of the States now confederated became convinced that the government of the United States had fallen into the hands of a sectional majority, who would pervert that most sacred of all trusts to the destruction of the rights which it was pledged to protect. They believed that to remain longer in the Union would subject them to a continuance of a disparaging discrimination, submission to which would be inconsistent with their welfare, and intolerable to a proud people. They therefore determined to sever its bonds, and establish a new confederacy for themselves.

The experiment instituted by our Revolutionary fathers, of

a voluntary union of sovereign States for purposes specified in a solemn compact, had been perverted by those who, feeling power and forgetting right, were determined to respect no law but their own will. *The government had ceased to answer the ends for which it was ordained and established.* To save ourselves from a revolution which, in its silent but rapid progress, was about to place us under *the despotism of numbers*, and to preserve in spirit, as well as in form, *a system of government we believe to be peculiarly fitted to our condition*, and full of promise for mankind, we determined to make a new association, composed of States *homogeneous in interest, in policy, and in feeling.*—*Extract from Jefferson Davis's Inaugural Address.*

Slaves with the Rebel Army. We clip the following from the New Orleans *Crescent*:—

"Tom, the slave of our citizen, James H. Phelps, took a fancy to go soldiering, and his master willingly gratified him, and Tom was engaged by Capt. Kountz of the De Soto Rifles to attend him through the war. There are hundreds of other slaves like Tom gone to kill the Yankees. Tom's highest ambition appears to be to kill a Yankee. He writes to his mother, who is owned in the family of Mr. Phelps, the letter below. We hope he will be gratified in hunting up and obtaining a Yankee's scalp:—

'Yorktown, Va., July 4, 1861.

Dear Mother,—I take this opportunity of writing to you to let you know that I am well and doing well, and I hope that this letter will find you as well as I am now in Yorktown. I will leave at 4 o'clock p. m. today for a scout about the woods for the Yankees. Well, we are only six miles from the Yankees at Young's Mill, where my captain is now, and I am going out to-day at 4 o'clock to find him. I left him at Warwick Court-House, nine miles from Yorktown. I came back to get some blankets, and then moved on to Young's Mill. We are looking out for a fight on the 5th of July by the 5th Regiment Louisiana volunteers. Give my love to Mistress and Master Jim Phelps, and to all of them in New Orleans. You must excuse this bad writing. I am writing in a hurry. have not time to write. I am about to leave for the Mill. So good by all. No more at present.

Your devoted son, THOMAS A. PHELPS.

P. S.—Good by to the white folks until I kill a Yankee. T. A. P.'"

TREASONABLE SOUTHERN PIETY. The *Southern Presbyterian* is edited by a Presbyterian minister, and is published at Columbia, S. C., the seat of the State College, and of the Presbyterian Theological Seminary. Its editorial columns bristle with lying paragraphs like these:—

"The phrensy of the North, demoniac in its wrath and its purposes against the South, seems to be unabated, and troops for our subjugation continue to be collected in larger numbers at Washington and central points in the Northern States. The fanatical leaders of the North are impatient at a moment's delay in the march of their legions into our borders, and their most prominent papers openly threaten Lincoln, if he falter an instant, that he will be deposed from his office, and the reins of power put into more faithful hands. To this length has the disorganization of the Northern mind already gone. Law and order, reason and common sense, have fled from the presence of the reign of terror which seems about to overthrow every vestige of free and constitutional government.

"The most brutal and blood-thirsty spirit towards the South prevails at the North. The purpose is openly avowed to plunder, devastate and destroy our country. Placards are put up in New York, calling for volunteers for the invasion of the South, with the heading 'Booty and Beauty.'

"The battle-cry through the North is, 'Overrun the South; raise a servile insurrection; proclaim freedom to the slaves; arm them against the whites; and wipe the accursed slavocracy from the face of the earth!'"

A correspondent of the same paper says:—

"*Hordes of Northern Goths and Vandals, savage as the barbarians of old*, inspired not with a mere lust of rapine, but with vindictive hate and fury, threaten to invade our land, to desecrate the temples of religion, to lay waste our peaceful homes, to murder and destroy our people, to summon our slaves to insurrection, and to make our country a desolation. And among those who encourage and applaud these ruthless designs of the infuriated North are our own ecclesiastical brethren, the venerable, pious, calm, moderate patriarchs of the Old Presbyterian Church! Surely madness is in their hearts. Surely this is the time foretold when it is said, 'Woe to the inhabiters of the earth and of the sea, for the devil is come down unto you, having great wrath, because he knoweth that he hath but a short time!'

"Nothing would satisfy the North but our implicit submission to be governed by it on its own terms and in its own way. And now they unanimously proclaim their purpose to compel us at the point of the sword to yield that submission; to make our land a desert, and our homes a desolation, if we will not. They will slaughter us at the cannon's mouth, or hang us on the gallows; they will burn us, and drown us, and sweep us from the face of the earth. But they will not allow us to be 'free and independent.'

"But, God help us, and we will! We desire not war. We have done everything possible to be done to avert it, except *submit.* And, if it must come, we can only meet it as it has often been met before by a brave and a Christian people. The threats of the North do not terrify us, fearful as they are. Their ferocious clamor for vengeance only nerves the Southern heart for resistance to the last extremity, and will convert every Southern man into a martyr."

COLUMBUS, (Ga.,) Sept. 17.

DEAR COUSIN,—I received your letter the other night, and I make haste to write you another. The war-dogs will be upon us, and that soon. Our Governor is making great preparation for coast defences. He has called out all the militia, and calls upon every one to be ready at a moment's notice. When I read your letter to Sis, and came to the part where you said *you would write me a letter in blood*, she shuddered, and said she did not like to hear such. But *I do*, and if I ever go to war, *I shall bring me a scalp home;* and if you have a fight, *I want you to send me one, and I will hang it up in my room, and gaze upon and pity the poor mortal that would dare fight against Southern chivalry.* I am all for the war, and mourn over my lot that I am not allowed to go; but soon eight months will pass away, and then I can go, if the war continues. I will be in, and I will show them what I can do. I pray not for the destruction of my enemies, but *would that I could shoot down six, and see them fall and hear their death-shriek, and then I would be satisfied.* I would then rest from the scenes of war, but not until every enemy is driven from our shores. But I hope I will have a hand in the show here at home, when they invade our State — the Empire State of the South. Times are very dull here. Sister is teaching school now, and she wrote you a letter the day before I received yours. May this find you still alive, and when the time comes for you to lay down your life in the cause of your country, may you lay it down to ascend to the right hand of Jesus Christ and of our Father, where there will be no more wars, or strife, or sorrow, or tears; and may we all be gathered around the Throne, where we will praise the Father, and the Son, and the Holy Ghost forever. Amen!

From your well-wishing cousin,

H. T. Everett.

To Arms! To Arms! Unless we win the battle, Virginia is really quite ruined. The people who will seize on her are relentless, coarse, greedy and bloody. They will pillage our houses, violate our women, insult and murder defenceless citizens. The truest patriots of the State, who have not had the good sense to get themselves bravely killed in some battle, will die by the hands of lawless and irresponsible ruffians, or on the gallows after mockery of trial, or drag out a poor and miserable remnant of life in exile. The land called Virginia will remain; but so changed, so utterly revolutionized, inhabited by a population sprung from such ruthless confiscations and proscriptions, that it will be not more recognizable than Italy after its partition between the Goths and the Vandals. To prevent the imminent wretchedness, the indescribable calamity that hangs over us, there is but one thing to do — and that is, to hurry up the troops to the places of rendezvous, and to concentrate the armies who must save us, if saved we can be. Virginia alone is perfectly able to turn the current of invasion; and she will do it perfectly well, if her force is handled with decision and intelligence. She can meet and beat an army of fifty thousand volunteers with absolute certainty; and that is more than the North can get here before the crisis of the danger has passed. — *Richmond Examiner.*

THE MULATTO VICE-PRESIDENT. The Memphis *Avalanche* has an article on the "mulatto" Vice-President of the North. It remarks: "We have only been able to account for the remarkable lukewarmness of Hannibal Hamlin, in regard to this abolition war, by attributing it to the general distrust of abolition sincerity entertained by his race. With a decided infusion of African blood in his veins, a fact never successfully controverted, we may suppose that he shares the sentiments and feelings of his African kin. Neither is it improbable that an instinctive sense of incongruity and impropriety of an individual of negro extraction ruling over white people induces his reticence and modesty. Every well-bred negro or mulatto would shrink from such an anomalous position as unbecoming; and Hannibal may be supposed to be well-bred, having received an education superior to that usually bestowed on free mulattoes."

THE spring of hope must now, with the Yankees, die upon the winter winds. Already the black flag has been hoisted upon the soil of South Carolina, and *war to the knife, and knife to the hilt, and thence to the shoulder*, been proclaimed by her noble sons as the only booty which Yankee hireling invaders shall receive at their hands. This is right. It is the only way to conquer a peace with a people so lost and degraded as those which compose the grand army of the rump government. We look anxiously for news from the sunny South; hopefully, prayerfully, with no misgivings. Now that the rallying-cry is, "No quarter to the invaders of our soil," may we not believe that the course inaugurated by South Carolina will be followed up by our whole army, and thus end the war? "So mote it be."—*Petersburg* (*Va.*) *Express.*

THE intelligence of yesterday, that *the myrmidons of Federal power* had advanced upon the soil of Virginia produced an electrifying effect in our community, and among the soldiery. Every eye brightened, and every heart beat high with stern delight that the hour of vengeance was at hand.—*Richmond Dispatch.*

ADDRESS TO THE PEOPLE OF GEORGIA.

Fellow-Citizens,—In a few days, the Provisional Government of the Confederate States will live only in history. With it we shall deliver up the trust we have endeavored to use for your benefit, to those more directly selected by yourselves. The public record of our acts is familiar to you, and requires no further explanation at our hands. Of those matters which policy has required to be secret, it would be improper now to speak. This address, therefore, will have no personal reference. We are well assured that there exists no necessity for us to arouse your patriotism, nor to inspire your confidence. We rejoice with you in the unanimity of our State, in its resolution and its hopes. And we are proud with you that Georgia has been "illustrated," and we doubt not will be illustrated again by her sons in our holy struggle. The first campaign is over; each party rests in place, while the winter's snow declares an armistice from on high. The results in the field are familiar to you, and we will not recount them. To some important facts we call your attention:—

First. The moderation of our own government and *the fanatical madness of our enemies* have dispersed all differences of opinion among our people, and united them forever in the war of independence. In a few border States, a waning opposition is giving way before the stern logic of daily developing facts. The world's history does not give a parallel instance of a revolution based upon such unanimity among the people.

Second. Our enemy has exhibited an energy, a perseverance, and an amount of resources which we had hardly expected, and a disregard of Constitution and laws (!!) which we can hardly credit. The result of both, however, is that power, which is the characteristic element of despotism, and renders it as formidable to its enemies as it is destructive to its subjects.

Third. An immense army has been organized for our destruction, which is being disciplined to the unthinking stolidity of regulars. With the exclusive possession of the seas, our enemy is enabled to throw upon the shores of every

State the nucleus of an army. And the threat is made, and doubtless the attempt will follow in early spring, to crush us with a giant's grasp by a simultaneous movement along our entire borders.

Fourth. With whatever alacrity our people may rush to arms, and with whatever energy our Government may use its resources, we cannot expect to cope with our enemy either in numbers, equipments or munitions of war. To provide against these odds, we must look to desperate courage, unflinching daring, and universal self-sacrifice.

Fifth. The prospect of foreign interference is at least a remote one, and should not be relied on. If it comes, let it be only auxiliary to our own preparations for freedom. To our God and ourselves alone we should look.

These are stern facts; perhaps some of them are unpalatable. But we are deceived in you if you would have us conceal them in order to deceive you. The only question for us and for you is, as a nation and individually, what have we to do? We answer,—

First. As a nation we should be united, forbearing to one another, frowning upon all factious opposition and censorious criticisms, and giving a trustful and generous confidence to those selected as our leaders in the camp and the council chamber.

Second. We should excite every nerve and strain every muscle of the body politic to maintain our financial and military healthfulness, and, by rapid aggressive action, make our enemies feel, at their own firesides, the horrors of a war brought on by themselves.

The most important matter for you, however, is your individual duty. What can you do?

The foot of the oppressor is on the soil of Georgia. *He comes with lust in his eye, poverty in his purse, and hell in his heart. He comes a robber and a murderer.* How shall you meet him? With the sword, at the threshold! *With death for him or for yourself!* But more than this—let every woman have a torch, every child a firebrand—let the loved homes of our youth be made ashes, and the fields of our heritage be made desolate. Let blackness and ruin mark your departing steps, if depart you must, and let a desert more terrible than Sahara welcome the Vandals. Let every city be levelled by the flame and every village be lost in ashes. Let your faithful slaves share your fortune and your crust. Trust wife and children to the sure refuge and protection of God—*preferring even for these loved ones the charnel-house as a home, than loathsome vassalage to a nation already sunk below the contempt of the civilized world.* This may be your terrible choice, and determine at once and without dissent as honor and patriotism and duty to God require.

Fellow-citizens, lull not yourselves into a fatal security. Be prepared for every contingency. This is our only hope for a sure and honorable peace. If our enemy was, to-day, convinced that the feast herein indicated would welcome him in every quarter of this Confederacy, *we know his base character* well enough to be assured that he would never come. Let, then, the smoke of your homes, fired by women's hands, tell the approaching foe that over sword and bayonet they will rush only to fire and ruin.

We have faith in God and faith in you. He is blind to every indication of Providence who has not seen an Almighty hand controlling the events of the past year. The wind, the wave, the cloud, the mist, the sunshine and the storm have all ministered to our necessities, and frequently succored us in our distresses. We deem it unnecessary to recount the numerous instances which have called forth our gratitude. We would join you in thanksgiving and praise. "If God be for us, who can be against us?"

Nor would we condemn your confident look to our armies, when they can meet a foe not too greatly their superior in numbers. The year past tells a story of heroism and success, of which our nation will never be ashamed. These considerations, however, should only stimulate us to greater deeds and nobler efforts. An occasional reverse we must expect—such as has depressed us within the last few days. This is only temporary.

We have no fears of the result—the final issue. You and we may have to sacrifice our lives in the holy cause; but our honor will be saved untarnished, and our children's children will rise up to call us "blessed."

HOWELL COBB, R. TOOMBS,
M. J. CRAWFORD, THOS. R. R. COBB.

The Hand-Writing on the Wall. The North is at blood-heat from Maine to Nebraska. Every city, village and county is in arms. One continuous roll of drums sweeps the land. They outnumber the South more than two to one. They boast of untold millions of wealth, and exhaustless provisions at command. They are armed and equipped; they have monopolized always the manufacture of arms on this continent; and, besides this, while they were professing peace two months ago to the South, they had an agent in Europe buying 500,000 more arms of the most approved pattern. These are being received by every steamer. And what is the spirit that moves the vast North? Revenge and hate stream through every column of their journals. Conciliation, peace and mercy are banished words. "War to the knife," "extermination of the rebels," "crush the traitors," are the common forms of their expression. The South is to be overrun and crushed forever; her proud spirit broken, her property confiscated, her families scattered and slaughtered, and then to remain, through all time, a dependency on the "free and sovereign" North. Powerful armies of fanatics and plunderers are to be quartered in our cities and towns in the South, dictating to us laws at the point of the bayonet, and the slaves to be turned loose with more than savage atrocity on helpless women and children. Every friend we had in the North is silenced, the entire press is against us, and the ministers of religion, without distinction, are praying for the "holy cause,"—the utter reduction of the rebels. At the bottom of all this lies the insane idea, held by many of the leaders, that it is their *religious duty* to exterminate slavery, and make the "Irrepressible-Conflict" doctrine universal. The men who have acted with and for the South,—Pierce, Buchanan, Fillmore, Cass, Everett and Dickinson,—all have bowed before the torrent of fanaticism; all have left us, and chime their voices in the fearful chorus of Northern indignation. Aged ministers of the gospel, presidents of colleges, and editors of religious newspapers,—all, without exception, so far as we know, urge on the maddened and bloody populace. The vast North staggers under its load of wrath, waiting only for orders from the usurper Lincoln to overwhelm the South with blood and chains.—*Nashville* (*Tenn.*) *paper*.

The Yankees are the lineal descendants of the Vi-Kings, the sea-rovers and land-robbers of Norway and Denmark. They retain all the qualities and characteristics of their illustrious ancestry. They are the best privateers, the best pirates, the best fillibusters, and the best kidnappers in the world. They are, besides, the wire-grass of nations, and gradually and insidiously worm themselves among the people of various countries, and cheat them out of their lands, when they are not strong enough to rob them of them.

Yet, they would have a monopoly of dishonesty, and insist that what is honorable and reputable in themselves, is highly unbecoming in other people. For a Yankee to be a sharp fellow and half a rogue is all right, for it is his *metier;* but the chivalrous and honorable Southron disgraces himself, in Yankee eyes, when he takes to Yankee ways. This is all perfectly right. Stealing, lying and cheating are creditable in a Yankee, disgraceful to a Southron. But retaliation is not theft, any more than killing, in self-defence, is murder.

The Yankee threatened, and is attempting to sack, plunder and burn our cities; to stir up our slaves to insurrection; to steal our lands, and to violate our women. When he had done all this, and not until he had done it, we turn round to him, and to make him stay his hand, propose to issue letters of marque and reprisal, to meet him on his favorite element, and to compete with him in his favorite and time-honored pursuit. Instead of admiring our fairness and our chivalry, and complimenting us on the occasion, he sets up a howl of abuse and indignation that pandemonium, let loose, could hardly emulate.—*Richmond Examiner.*

Eternal Hate to the North. The *National Intelligencer* says a subscriber writes from Athens, Georgia, May 8, 1861, as follows:—"There is now *no Union or reconstruction* party in the South. My business brings me in intimate connection with the best men of this State, also with the masses. *One universal remark is, 'undying hate to the North.'* I have been for the Union, but now I am for *eternal* hate to the North. I will advocate, at the next Legislature, a bill making it penal to purchase anything made at the North, except munitions of war and things taken in war. This is no personal feeling on my *individual* part, but the feeling of the masses, and I only write to you that you may honestly know how the people stand. The whole State is in arms, and if we fail, many persons propose to desolate the country and retreat; and if that will not do, to *offer* the country to England as a colony. Anybody, anything, rather than the North. This is the universal opinion of the people. I lately met the prominent men of the State at the executive meeting of the Agricultural Society of the State. We gave all our cash ($4500) to the State; we sold some silver plate for the same purpose. We cut up our large canvass tents to make soldiers' tents, and most of the members present said they belonged to military companies. An old man, seventy-two years of age, who was a sergeant at Lundy's Lane and Chippewa, has joined a company and is now in Virginia, with *three* sons, all in the Georgia army. I mention this that you may know the eternal hate which inspires our people."

YANKEE "LIONS" AND SPIES. It will scarcely be believed abroad that, in times of flagrant war, while the soil of Virginia is pressed by the foot of *a blood-thirsty and murderous foe*, the most tender and unceasing attentions are yet offered in Richmond, not only to the *vagrant Yankees* who have come here on suspicious errands, but actually to those *whose mission toward us was to cut our throats, burn our houses, and defile our families with the brutal lusts of war*. The evidences of this disposition are patent and brazen enough. The case of Dr. King, a Rhode Islander, who was permitted to come here and take away a son, who had been taken as our prisoner in the battle at Manassas, and to pass his time here in receiving calls from and paying visits to certain social pretenders and jackals who made a "lion" of him, is an illustration of the disgrace that is fastening upon our city, not only for the laxity of the authorities of the government, but for the subserviency and social demoralization of its manners.

The half has not been told of the exploitation of the Yankee family of Kings in the society of Richmond. We are credibly informed that the young cut-throat and murderer, who was taken fighting against us at Manassas, was actually taken from the hospital and tenderly nursed in the family of a physician in this city. Could not these good Samaritans have found some poor Confederate soldier languishing in the hospitals, an object for their solicitude and kindness, into whose wounds they might have poured oil, rather than the Yankee whom they took into their family circle to nurse, to pet, and to restore to his New England home?—*Richmond Examiner.*

Choice Extracts. The following choice extracts are taken from the Richmond *Dispatch:*—

"Preparing with rapid strides to meet *the Illinois baboon* and his co-workers of iniquity on the borders of our once happy old State, to welcome them with 'bloody hands to hospitable graves.' * * * Stepped forward to drive back the half-starved Lincolnites, who, with open mouths, are seeking to devour us with eager avidity. * * * Well, let them come—those minions of the North. We'll meet them in a way they least expect; we'll glut our carrion crows with their beastly carcasses. Yes, from the peaks of the Blue Ridge to tide-water, will we strew our plains, and leave their bleaching bones to enrich our soil. * * * Colonel Corcoran has found it very easy to swallow an oath, binding him to come to Virginia to cut our throats, and steal the poor negro from his comfortable home. * * * Lincoln seems to still persist in refusing not only Confederate States' ships permission to pass Old Point, but he demurs in granting British ships that privilege, and in all probability will continue to do so until the Old Lion gets fully mad, springs to his feet, and brings a roar that will make *the Ape* quake with terror, and his rotten fleet return home. * * * No honest man or nation can do otherwise than execrate the whole batch of politicians, spawned into existence from Black Republican stools. * * * They are all in good spirits, and determined to give Old Abe's canailles a warm reception, if they come to invade the Valley."

PROCLAMATION OF GOVERNOR PICKENS. On the 26th of April, 1861, the Governor of South Carolina issued his Proclamation "to the volunteer regiments of the State," which concludes with the following flourish: —

"Soldiers of South Carolina! hold yourselves in readiness to march at the word to the tomb of Washington, and swear that no *Northern Goths and Vandals* shall ever desecrate its sacred precincts, and that you will make of it an American Mecca, to which the votaries of freedom and independence, from the South, shall make their pilgrimage through all time to come. Let the sons of South Carolina answer to the call from the sons of Col. Howard, who led the Maryland line in triumph over the bloody battle-field of Cowpens. Let them know that we will return that blood with full interest, and let them feel that they are now, as they were then, our brothers. March to Virginia, and lay your heads upon the bosom of this mother of States, and hear her great heart beat with new impulses for a renewed and glorious independence.

"Surely the good and the virtuous of the Northern States cannot sanction the lawless and brutal despotism now inaugurated at Washington.

"Be ready! Stand by your arms,—mark time to the tap of independence, and at the word, march forward and onward to the Borders. Our glorious old sister, North Carolina, is with you, and her freemen are in arms. Join them in the struggle for defence; and let tyrants know that there are men who can make them hear the ring and feel the weight of Southern steel. I shall endeavor not to expose our own State, and shall only march you beyond our borders under pressing emergency; but wherever the Confederate flag floats, there too is our country, now and forever.

F. F. PICKENS."

PREMATURE BOASTING. Among the papers found on the Pea Ridge battle-ground was a letter from a Texas captain to his wife, written just before the battle, in which the writer said:—"Thank God, dear Mary, we've got the Yankees in a trap at last. They cannot escape us now. We have more than twice as many men as they, and we have a plan to cut them off, and annihilate them. Before a week has passed, you will hear of a terrible defeat of the Lincolnites, such an one as will offset to some extent our mortifying surrender at Donelson. We are certain of success, and I hope I will be able to bring five or six Yankee prisoners to Galveston next summer. The Northern men will not fight when they can avoid it; but we intend to make them this time, or *cut their throats*. The coming battle will free Arkansas and Missouri from the invaders, and we will then march on to St. Louis, and take that Abolition city, and give the oppressed Southerners there an opportunity to be free once more. We hear that we would be welcomed in St. Louis by at least 50,000 people, who have long suffered from *the tyranny of the mercenary Dutch*."

WHAT THE WAR IS, SOUTH. That Northern readers may see a little of the spirit of the South, we publish an extract from the Richmond *Dispatch*, and we could fill a volume every day with similar extracts from the Southern press:—

"It is not a war of punctilio between sovereigns; nor of conflicting interests between rival nations—admitting of adjustment and compromise. It is a war of fanaticism and subjugation on the part of the North; *of scorn and contemptuous hatred on the part of the South.*

"These angry passions are uncontrollable, transporting and irrepressible. The South would sacrifice everything it holds dear, before it would succumb to the authority of *the despised North;* and the North will forget all schemes of gain, and throw its ledgers into the fire, to indulge its fanatical hatred of slavery, to 'crush out' the slaveholder. * * *

"We cannot build conclusions in regard to the duration of this war upon considerations of interests. *The foes we have to fight are madmen.* The madness which we combat is the same madness which has for thirty years been abusing and villifying the best customers of the people it possessed, which has spread discord and hatred throughout the land, which has diabolically cut the bonds of Union, and pulled down the pillars of the fairest government that ever blessed mankind."

CHALLENGE TO THE SOLDIERS OF MASSACHUSETTS. The following document (says the Boston *Traveller*) was received at this office by mail. The envelope bore the post-mark of Charleston, S. C., and we therefore have no doubt that it is genuine:—

"CHARLESTON, S. C., April 19, 1861.

To the Editors of the Boston Traveller:

"GENTLEMEN,—On behalf of the South Carolina Volunteers, I am deputed to request Gov. Andrew, of Massachusetts, through you, that the military contingent of your State be sent to South Carolina. In making this request, I assure you I but express the wish of every man, woman and child in our State. We number about 10,000 men, well armed and accoutred, and anxious for a fight, and cordially invite *any number* from your section to give us a meeting. Do not, however, send them in the fleet that appeared off Charleston harbor during the bombardment of Fort Sumter, for fear their timidity will interfere with their landing. Send all Massachusetts men—none from Pennsylvania, for the regiment of that State *flunked* at Cerro Gordo; nor from New York, for at Cherubusco, (although they claimed and received the right from the Palmetto Regiment,) at the first fire, the gallant New Yorkers fell back, and hid behind a barn; nor from Indiana, for at Palo Alto, the *nimble* regiment from that State fled in inglorious confusion. Send your Sumners, your Wilsons, your Burlingames, and a host of similar notables, and we pledge our honors, our lives, and all that we hold sacred, that none others but the Palmetto Boys shall interfere with them. We want them exclusively for our own use.

"This request is made in good faith, and on signifying your acceptance of our offer, every arrangement will be made to give you a safe passport to our shores.

ON BEHALF OF THE S. C. VOLUNTEERS."

THE DRUNKEN MUTINEERS. We would enter into no negotiation now with Lincoln, unless a cannon were planted behind us, prepared to sweep him from the earth, upon the first indication of perfidy. This is the flag of truce under whose protection we would trust ourselves. None other would be heeded by Abraham Lincoln.

This same man is engaged now in another fraud. He tells us that *the thirty thousand mercenaries that defile the Capital* are for its defence—nothing more. Who believes him? Not we. They are designed for offensive operations. They are intended to menace Virginia, and will make a descent somewhere upon our soil. Very well. Let *the drunken mutineers at Washington* drive on in their crazy craft. The breakers are ahead, and they must evince more statesmanship than they have yet indicated if they weather the storm that is gathering.—*Lynchburgh Virginian.*

MORE SOUTHERN RASCALITY. The following is a copy of a letter received by a manufacturer of boots and shoes in Haverhill:—

"RICHMOND, Va., April 18, 1861.

"*Messrs.* ——, *Haverhill, Mass.:*

"Owing to the declaration of *war* against our beloved South, and the necessity of our arming and fighting, instead of pursuing the peaceful avocations of commerce, we have given up ourselves fully and freely to the work before us, and our resources are to be held at the disposal of the State until the issue is finally determined, when, if we have sufficient availabilities or assets left to meet our liabilities, it shall be done.

"But untilt his fratricidal war *is closed*, we shall decline paying any of our debts due to parties in the North, where they have drawn the sword against us. Hence the protest of our note in your favor this day, *which we have the funds in bank to meet.* Very truly yours,

(Signed) WESTON & WILLIAMS."

This is an exact copy, underlined as they underlined it. They owe different parties here to the amount of several thousand dollars.—*Boston Journal.*

Is the North peopled with Christians or with savages? Is the light that shone from Calvary's bloody summit extinguished, and are our Northern foes only guided by the dark and lurid flame that pilots devils to their carnivals? Has the Congress of Hell had its session, and have they commissioned all the legions of the damned to demonize our enemies? Has Lucifer given a furlough to all his infernal cohorts? Has he established his church in every Black Republican's heart, and has he ordained Belial and Moloch his high priests? Are we to have war with men or with devils? These questions must be answered. Our implacable foes, goaded on by a hatred that is remorseless and unrelenting, because *they* have insulted and injured *us*, have already answered them. They have inaugurated a war of extermination—a war in which no mercy is to be shown or quarter given. Let it be so! The South has never asked a favor of her enemies. She asks none now.—*Vicksburg Whig.*

VIRGINIA is invaded. The horde of thieves, robbers and assassins in the pay of Abraham Lincoln, commonly known as the army of the United States, have rushed into the peaceful streets of a chief city of the State, and stained the hearth of Virginian homes with the blood of her sons.

One trait of true heroism has signalized this unhappy affair. A citizen of Alexandria, named Jackson, lacked the prudence to haul down the flag of his country, which streamed over his dwelling. That band of execrable cut-throats and jail-birds, known as the "Zouaves," of New York, under *the chief of all scoundrels, called Col. Ellsworth,* surrounded the house of this Virginian, and broke open the door to tear down the flag of the South. The courageous owner of that house neither fled nor submitted. He met the favorite hero of every Yankee there in his hall, he alone, against thousands, and shot him through the heart!—*Richmond Examiner.*

www.ingramcontent.com/pod-product-compliance
Lightning Source LLC
LaVergne TN
LVHW011123110826
845150LV00008B/2232

* 9 7 8 1 4 1 8 1 9 5 3 1 1 *